The PRAYING WITH series

PRAYING WITH SAINT AUGUSTINE
Introduction by Murray Watts

PRAYING WITH SAINT FRANCIS
Introduction by David Ford

PRAYING WITH HIGHLAND CHRISTIANS
Introduction by Sally Magnusson

PRAYING WITH THE NEW TESTAMENT
Introduction by Joyce Huggett

PRAYING WITH SAINT TERESA
Introduction by Elaine Storkey

PRAYING WITH THE JEWISH TRADITION
Introduction by Lionel Blue

PRAYING WITH THE OLD TESTAMENT
Introduction by Richard Holloway

PRAYING WITH THE ORTHODOX TRADITION
Preface by Kallistos Ware

PRAYING WITH THE ENGLISH HYMN WRITERS
Compiled and Introduced by Timothy Dudley-Smith

PRAYING WITH THE ENGLISH MYSTICS
Compiled and Introduced by Jenny Robertson

PRAYING WITH THE ENGLISH TRADITION
Compiled and Introduced by Margaret Pawley

PRAYING WITH THE ENGLISH POETS
Compiled and Introduced by Ruth Etchells

PRAYING WITH THE MARTYRS
Compiled by Duane Arnold

PRAYING WITH

John Donne & George Herbert

Compiled and Edited by
Duane W. H. Arnold

Introduction by
The Rt Revd Richard Harries
Bishop of Oxford

First published 1991
Triangle
SPCK
Holy Trinity Church
Marylebone Road
London NW1 4DU

British Library Cataloguing in Publication Data
Donne, John, *1572–1631*
  Praying with Donne and Herbert.
  I. Title   II. Herbert, George, *1593–1633*
  III. Arnold, Duane W. H.
  821.3

  ISBN 0-281-04552-6

Typeset by Rowland Phototypesetting Ltd
Bury St Edmunds, Suffolk
Printed in Great Britain by
BPCC Hazell Books
Aylesbury, Bucks

Contents

PROLOGUE

CONFESSION AND CONTRITION

SUPPLICATION AND PRESERVATION

ADORATION AND THANKSGIVING

EPILOGUE

To
John G. B. Andrew

Yet in thy temple thou dost him afford
This glorious and transcendent place,
To be a window, through thy grace.

Introduction

Shortly after I began to read Theology at Cambridge an English student introduced me to George Herbert and John Donne. In the course of her studies she had been overwhelmed by George Herbert's 'Love III' and John Donne's 'Batter my heart, three person'd God'. The poems had a similar impact on me as they have had on so many. The first describes how 'Love bade me welcome: yet my soul drew back'; still love, sensitive and persistent, overcomes George Herbert's self-doubts so that he comes to sit at table with divine love. John Donne's poem, on the other hand, has a sense of contained violence, as evidenced by its first line 'Batter my heart'. John Donne is conscious that it needs all God's force to overcome his human reluctance and recalcitrance: aware of the strength of human lust, he knows his desperate need for an overpowering grace.

> . . . For I
> Except you enthral me, never shall be free,
> Nor ever chaste, except you ravish me.

After a brilliant academic career George Herbert became Public Orator at Cambridge, all set for advancement at Court. His poetry reflects his sense of being courtier to a divine king, reverent, humble, with all the proper courtesies expressed in spirit as well as in letter. The note which sounds through his poetry more than any other is that of praise. A poet of the following century, Christopher Smart, once wrote:

Praise above all – for praise prevails;
Heap up the measure, load the scales,
And good to goodness add.

It is a sentiment that characterises Herbert's poetry. The human spirit is, sadly, often niggardly and begrudging. We withhold praise where praise is due, we criticise rather than admire. As Christopher Smart put it in the same poem ('A Song to David'), 'peevish obloquy degrades'. To this is added the further difficulty that we find it hard to focus on the eternal, infinite and invisible God enough for praise to be real. But we can enlarge our own soul by entering into the tradition of praise which is so much part of our inheritance. George Herbert stands with so many of the psalms: 'Praise the Lord O my soul, all that is within me praise his holy name'. We ourselves may not feel very much like praising and we might find great difficulty in grasping what it is to praise God, but we can allow George Herbert to take hold of us and lift us beyond where we are.

Not surprisingly praise in George Herbert is most intimately linked to the theme of music. Music and praise for him are almost inseparable. The number of musical references even in this short collection is considerable.

Awake, my lute, and struggle for thy part
With all thy art.
                                                        'Easter'

Both George Herbert and John Donne originally wanted to make their way in the secular world, in service of the king. Yet, thank God, this did not work out. How wasted both of them would have been as ordinary politicians or diplomats. The one was made to be a pastor and poet, the other a preacher and poet. God used the twin reins of success and failure until they found their proper calling.

Nevertheless, the poems of both of them witness to a continuing struggle between human desires and submission to divine grace. It is this which gives the poems their sense of controlled strength and disciplined passion, even if for our taste the emphasis upon guilt, sin and judgement seems overdone. But that is how they felt and our own complacency is hardly to be trusted as a surer guide. John Donne had to struggle not only with his worldly ambitions but with his sexual passions. As a young man he wrote some of the finest love poetry in the language. He was conscious of:

Being sacrilegiously
Half wasted with youth's fires, of pride and lust.

Donne's worldly prospects diminished after his clandestine marriage and subsequent disgrace. His hardships ended only when he became ordained and, in 1621, Dean of St. Paul's. But then he became severely ill, this giving rise to some of his best known pieces both in poetry and prose. He grappled with his sickness as a visitation from God and he reflected much on death as he himself became conscious that his life was drawing to an end.

Whilst Donne's writing can be much appreciated

for its own sake it also has another lesson for us as far as prayer is concerned. He encourages us to bring our whole self before God, all our passions and disquiet, our fear, our loathing and longing alike. If our relationship with God is to be real, then we must be real before God, bringing him the person we really are and not a polite pretence. Donne certainly gives us the incentive to do that, as he does to persist in our struggle to bring the whole of our life under God's graciousness.

Both writers are very modern in being anguished from time to time that God seems impervious to their prayers, absent or indifferent. Neither had an easy pilgrimage. Has anyone ever?

Like all writers their public esteem has varied. But they have never fallen totally out of favour and in our own century, particularly through the influence of people like T.S. Eliot and F.R. Leavis they have never been more widely appreciated. So many of their poems are in the form of prayers, a dialogue between the soul and God. They help us to take up the same dialogue, inspiring us with language that is at once beautiful, heartfelt and down to earth.

Richard Harries
Oxford

Life Sketches

John Donne and George Herbert

John Donne (1572–1631), whose poetry and prayers are a treasured legacy of the Anglican Church, and whose career reached up to the high position of the Dean of St Paul's Cathedral, London, was born into a Roman Catholic family distantly related to Sir Thomas More. Brought up in the 'old religion', Donne nevertheless entered Hart Hall, Oxford, in 1584. He left Oxford in 1587 to study at Trinity College, Cambridge and, in 1592, entered Lincoln's Inn to study law. Although he renounced the Roman Catholic faith at some point after this time and entered the Church of England, as late as 1617 his literary work still betrays an ambivalent attitude towards the claims of Anglicanism.

In part, this ambivalence may stem from an early career which was both reckless and uncertain. Set upon a course of secular success, Donne accompanied Essex and Raleigh in the expeditions to Cadiz in 1596 and to the Azores in 1597, during which time he wrote much of his secular poetry. He became secretary to Sir Thomas Egerton, Keeper of the Great Seal, in 1598, but was dismissed and briefly imprisoned four years later after secretly marrying his master's niece, Ann More, in 1601. Released from confinement, with no money and a growing family, Donne accepted an appointment under Thomas (afterwards Bishop) Morton to write a series of anti-Roman Catholic polemics which appeared in 1610–11.

By 1615, following his failure to secure a secular position of prominence and, so Donne claimed, a lengthy struggle of conscience, he accepted the direction of King James I to enter the priesthood of the Church of England. Immediately appointed as a Royal Chaplain, Donne held several charges in quick succession until, in 1621, he was named to the deanship of St Paul's Cathedral. Donne's last years, mainly spent in study and the preparation of sermons, which won him popular acclaim, also produced some of his greatest poetry.

Characterised by some as merely a 'careerist', Donne nevertheless produced some of the finest essays, sermons and poems of a century famed for its writers, poets and preachers. His early passionate and erotic works were a counterpoint to the intense religious devotion evident in his later writings. Many of his poems may properly be thought of as prayers in verse. The many facets of his life — exaltation, defeat, sadness (especially the death of his wife in 1617) and illness in the later years – are captured in the vigorous writings which are as vivid today as ever. The prayers included in *Devotions upon Emergent Occasions*, written following a serious illness in 1623, betray the conflict of a life that was often starkly pessimistic, caught between earth and heaven, fleshly desire and spiritual aspiration. Many of these appear in this book. Donne's prayers and poems have tremendous power to speak directly to us.

Though he lived at the same time, George Herbert (1593–1633) offers a telling contrast to Donne. The son of Lady Magdalen Herbert (to whom Donne addressed his *Holy Sonnets*) and the younger brother of the philosopher Lord Herbert of Cherbury, George Herbert was educated at Westminster School and Trinity College, Cambridge. His musical ability and classical scholarship enabled him to obtain a fellowship at Trinity in 1614. Six years later, Herbert became the Public Orator of the university which increased the favour he enjoyed at Court. Although Herbert's life seemed set upon a course of worldly advancement, the death of James I brought his secular ambitions to an end, while his close friendship with Nicholas Ferrar (the founder of the community at Little Gidding) encouraged him to seek Holy Orders. His church career began in 1626 and he was ordained a priest in 1630. William Laud, who later became the Archbishop of Canterbury, persuaded him to accept a living as the parish priest of Bemerton in Wiltshire, near Salisbury, where he lived and worked for the remaining years of his life. His time at Bemerton was marked by piety, zeal, and a humble devotion to his duties as a priest.

Known during his life as 'Holy George Herbert', it was said that 'next to Christianity itself, he loved the English Church'. In his life and written work, Herbert was the embodiment of the Laudian High Church party's challenge to the puritans, emphasising as he did the value of regular daily prayer and worship, and inspiring his parishioners to this. His prose work, *A Priest to the Temple; or the Country Parson*, provided an outline of pastoral theology and shows the life of a scholarly priest, temperate, careful for his flock, and devoted to prayer. His poems, prayers and well-loved hymns, celebrate the Church as Christ's bride, made more beautiful with the ornaments of faith and praise. As with Donne, many of his poems are prayers. Though not without his own elements of doubt and melancholy, Herbert is perhaps of all English poets the best able to convey a deep and essentially simple Christian faith.

In one letter from Donne to Herbert, the Dean of St Paul's sent along his personal seal to the rector of Bemerton. Upon the seal was engraved an anchor – the anchor of faith, a symbol of Christian commitment during times of uncertainty. Although different in their lives, careers, inclinations and styles of expression, the anchor of faith perhaps best symbolises that common commitment which unites the prayers and aspirations of John Donne and George Herbert and bids us to pray with them.

PROLOGUE

The Parson Praying

The country parson, when he is to read divine services, composeth himself to all possible reverence; lifting up his heart and hands, and eyes, and using all other gestures which may express a hearty and unfeigned devotion. This he doth, first, as being truly touched and amazed with the Majesty of God, before whom he then presents himself; yet not as himself alone, but as presenting with himself the whole congregation, whose sins he then bears, and brings with his own to the heavenly altar to be bathed, and washed in the sacred laver of Christ's blood. Secondly, as this is the true reason of his inward fear, so he is content to express this outwardly to the utmost of his power; that being first affected himself, he may affect also his people, knowing that no sermon moves them so much to a reverence, which they forget again, when they come to pray, as a devout behaviour in the very act of praying. Accordingly his voice is humble, his words treatable, and slow; yet not so slow neither, as to let the fervency of the supplicant hang and die between speaking, but with a grave liveliness, between fear and zeal, pausing yet pressing, he performs his duty. Besides his example, he having often instructed his people how to carry themselves in divine service, exacts of them all possible reverence, by no means enduring either talking, or sleeping, or gazing, or leaning, or half-kneeling, or any undutiful behaviour in them, but causing them, when they sit, or stand, or kneel, to do all in a straight and steady posture, as attending to what is done in the church, and every òne, man, and child, answering aloud both Amen, and all other answers, which are on the clerk's and people's part to answer; which answers also are to be done not in a huddling, or slubbering fashion, gaping, or scratching the head, or spitting even in the midst of their answer, but gently and pausably, thinking what they say; so that while they answer, [Glory be to the Father, and to the Son, and to the Holy Ghost] As it was in the beginning, [is now, and ever shall be: world without end. Amen], they meditate as they speak, that God hath ever had his people, that have glorified him as well as now, and that he shall have so forever. And the like in other answers. This is that which the Apostle calls a reasonable service (Rom. 12), when we speak not as parrots, without reason, or offer up such sacrifices as they did of old, which was of beasts devoid of reason; but when we use our reason, and apply our powers to the service of him that gives them. If there be any of the gentry or nobility of the parish, who sometimes make it a piece of state not to come at the beginning of service with their poor neighbours, but at mid-prayers, both to their own loss, and of theirs also who gaze upon them when they come in, and neglect the present service of God, he by no means suffers it, but after divers gentle admonitions, if they persevere, he causes them to be presented:[1] or if the poor churchwardens be affrighted with their greatness, notwithstanding his instruction that they ought not to be so, but even to let the world sink, so they do their duty, he present them himself, only

4

protesting to them, that not any ill will draws him to it, but the debt and obligation of his calling, being to obey God rather than men.

GEORGE HERBERT
The Country Parson

CONFESSION AND CONTRITION

Come, my Way, my Truth, my Life:
Such a Way, as gives us breath:
Such a Truth, as ends all strife:
Such a Life, as killeth death.

Such a Way, as Gives Us Breath

THAT WE MAY CHANGE

That we may change to evenness
This intermitting aguish Piety
That snatching cramps of wickedness
And Apoplexies of fast sin, may die;
That music of thy promises,
Not threats in thunder may
Awaken us to our just offices;
What in thy book, thou dost, or creatures say,
That we may hear, Lord hear us, when we
pray.

JD

CHURCH-LOCK AND KEY

I know it is my sin, which locks thine ears,
                    And binds thy hands,
Out-crying my requests, drowning my tears;
Or else the chillness of my faint demands.

But as cold hands are angry with the fire,
                    And mend it still;
So I do lay the want of my desire,
Not on my sins, or coldness, but thy will.

Yet hear, O God, only for his blood's sake
                    Which pleads for me:
For though sins plead too, yet like stones they
    make
His blood's sweet current much more loud to
    be.

                                        GH

THE SINS OF MY YOUTH

O eternal, and most gracious God, though thou knowest all my sins, yet thou knowest them not to my comfort, except thou know them by my telling them to thee; how shall I bring to thy knowledge by that way, those sins, which I my self know not?

If I accuse my self of original sin, wilt thou ask me if I know what original sin is? I know not enough of it to satisfy others, but I know enough to condemn my self, and to solicit thee.

If I confess to thee the sins of my youth, wilt thou ask me if I know what those sins were? I know them not so well as to name them all, nor am sure to live hours enough to name them all (for I did them then, faster than I can speak them now, when every thing that I did, conduced to some sin), but I know them so well, as to know, that nothing but thy mercy is so infinite as they.

If the naming of sins, of thought, word, and deed, of sin of omission, and of action, of sins against thee, against my neighbour, and against my self; of sin unrepented, and sins relapsed into after repentence; of sins of ignorance, and sins against the testimony of my conscience; of sins against thy commandments, sins against thy Son's prayer, and sins against our own creed; of sins against the laws of that Church, and sins against the laws of that state, in which thou hast given me my station; if the naming of these sins reach not home to all mine, I know what will. O Lord, pardon me all those sins, which thy Son Christ Jesus suffered for, who suffered for all the sins of all the world; for there is no

sin amongst all those which had not been my sin, if
thou hadst not been my God, and antedated me a
pardon in thy preventing grace.

JD

GRIEF

Oh who will give me tears? Come all ye
   springs,
Dwell in my head and eyes: come clouds, and
   rain:
My grief hath need of all the watery things,
That nature hath produced. Let every vein
Suck up a river to supply mine eyes,
My weary weeping eyes too dry for me,
Unless they get new conduits, new supplies
To bear them out, and with my state agree.
What are two shallow fords, two little spouts
Of a less world? The greater is but small,
A narrow cupboard for my griefs and doubts,
Which want provision in the midst of all.
Verses, ye are too fine a thing, too wise
For my rough sorrows: cease, be dumb and
   mute,
Give up your feet and running to mine eyes,
And keep your measures for some lover's lute,
Whose grief allows him music and a rhyme:
For mine excludes both measure, tune, and
   time.
        Alas, my God!

                         GH

SIN'S ROUND

Sorry I am, my God, sorry I am,
That my offences course it in a ring.
My thoughts are working like a busy flame,
Until their cockatrice[2] they hatch and bring:
And when they once have perfected their
  draughts,
My words take fire from my inflamèd thoughts.

My words take fire from my inflamèd thoughts,
Which spit it forth like the Sicilian hill.[3]
They vent the wares, and pass them with their
  faults,
And by their breathing ventilate the ill.
But words suffice not, where are lewd
  intentions:
My hands do join to finish the inventions.

My hands do join to finish the inventions:
And so my sins ascend three stories high,
As Babel grew, before there were dissensions.
Yet ill deeds loiter not: for they supply
New thoughts of sinning: wherefore, to my
  shame,
Sorry I am, my God, sorry I am.

GH

A SEA IN MY SOUL

O eternal, and most gracious God, having married this soul and this body in me, I humbly beseech thee, that my soul may look, and make her use of thy merciful proceedings towards my bodily restitution, and go the same way to a spiritual.

I am come by thy goodness, to the use of thine ordinary means for my body, to wash away those peccant humours, that endangered it. I have, O Lord, a river in my body, but a sea in my soul, and a sea swollen into the depth of a deluge, above the sea. Thou hast raised up certain hills in me heretofore, by which I might have stood safe, from these inundations of sin . . . and to the top of all these hills thou hast brought me heretofore; but this deluge, this inundation, is got above all my hills; and I have sinned and sinned, and multiplied sin to sin, after all these thy assistances against sin, and where is there water enough to wash away this deluge?

There is a red sea, greater than this ocean; and there is a little spring, through which this ocean, may power itself into that red sea. Let thy Spirit of true contrition and sorrow pass all my sins through these eyes, into the wounds of thy Son, and I shall be clean, and my soul so much better purged than my body, as it is ordained for a better, and a longer life.

JD

15

DENIAL

When my devotions could not pierce
      Thy silent ears;
Then was my heart broken, as was my verse:
      My breast was full of fears
          And disorder.

My bent thoughts, like a brittle bow,
      Did fly asunder;
Each took his way; some would to pleasures go,
      Some to the wars and thunder
          Of alarms.

As good go anywhere, they say,
      As to benumb
Both knees and heart, in crying night and day,
      Come, come, my God, O come,
          But no hearing.

Oh that thou shouldst give dust a tongue
      To cry to thee,
And then not hear it crying! all day long
      My heart was in my knee,
          But no hearing.

Therefore my soul lay out of sight,
      Untuned, unstrung:
My feeble spirit, unable to look right,
      Like a nipped blossom, hung
          Discontented.

Oh cheer and tune my heartless breast,
       Defer no time;
That so thy favours granting my request,
       They and my mind may chime,
              And mend my rhyme.

GH

DISCIPLINE

Throw away thy rod,
Throw away thy wrath:
      Oh my God,
Take the gentle path.

For my heart's desire
Unto thine is bent:
      I aspire
To a full consent.

Not a word or look
I affect to own,
      But by book,
And thy book alone.

Though I fail, I weep:
Though I halt in pace,
      Yet I creep
To the throne of grace.

Then let wrath remove;
Love will do the deed:
      For with love
Stony hearts will bleed.

Love is swift of foot;
Love's a man of war,
      And can shoot,
And can hit from far.

Who can 'scape his bow?
That which wrought on thee,
       Brought thee low,
Needs must work on me.

Throw away thy rod;
Though man frailties hath,
       Thou art God:
Throw away thy wrath.

GH

THY MERCY

O Lord, I most humbly acknowledge and confess, that by thy mercy I have a sense of thy justice; for not only those afflictions with which it pleasest thee to exercise me, awaken me to consider how terrible thy severe justice is; but even the rest and security which thou affordest me, puts me often into fear, that thou reservest and sparest me for a greater measure of punishment.

O Lord, I most humbly acknowledge and confess, that I have understood sin, by understanding thy laws and judgements; but have done against thy known and revealed will. Thou hast set up many candlesticks, and kindled many lamps in me; but I have either blown them out, or carried them to guide me in forbidden ways. Thou hast given me a desire of knowledge, and some means to it, and some possession of it; and I have armed my self with thy weapons against thee.

Yet, O God, have mercy upon me, for thine own sake have mercy upon me. Let not sin and me be able to exceed thee, nor to defraud thee, nor to frustrate thy purposes. But let me, in despite of me, be of so much use to thy glory, that by thy mercy to my sin, other sinners may see how much sin thou canst pardon.

JD

BITTERSWEET

Ah my dear angry Lord,
Since thou does love, yet strike;
Cast down, yet help afford;
Sure I will do the like.

I will complain, yet praise;
I will bewail, approve:
And all my sour-sweet days
I will lament, and love.

GH

SIN

Lord, with what care hast thou begirt us round!
  Parents first season us: then schoolmasters
  Deliver us to laws; they send us bound
To rules of reason, holy messengers,
Pulpits and Sundays, sorrow dogging sin,
  Afflictions sorted, anguish of all sizes,
  Fine nets and strategems to catch us in,
Bibles laid open, millions of surprises,
Blessings beforehand, ties of gratefulness,
  The sound of glory ringing in our ears:
  Without, our shame; within, our consciences;
Angels and grace, eternal hopes and fears.
  Yet all these fences and their whole array
  One cunning bosom-sin blows quite away.

GH

Such a Truth, as Ends all Strife

THE ALTAR

A broken ALTAR, Lord, thy servant rears,
Made of a heart, and cemented with tears:
Whose parts are as thy hand did frame;
No workman's tool hath touch'd the same.
A HEART alone
Is such a stone,
As nothing but
Thy pow'r doth cut.
Wherefore each part
Of my hard heart
Meets in this frame,
To praise thy Name.
That if I chance to hold my peace,
These stones to praise thee may not cease.
Oh let thy blessed SACRIFICE be mine,
And sanctify this ALTAR to be thine.

GH

REPENTANCE

Lord, I confess my sin is great;
Great is my sin. Oh! gently treat
With thy quick flower, thy momentary bloom;
        Whose like still pressing
        Is one undressing,
A steady aiming at a tomb.

Man's age is two hours' work, or three:
Each day doth round about us see.
Thus are we to delights: but we are all
        To sorrows old,
        If life be told
From what life feeleth, Adam's fall.

Oh let thy height of mercy then
Compassionate short-breathèd men.
Cut me not off for my most foul transgression:
        I do confess
        My foolishness;
My God, accept of my confession.

Sweeten at length this bitter bowl,
Which thou hast poured into my soul;
Thy wormword turn to health, winds to fair
   weather:
        For if thou stay,
        I and this day,
As we did rise, we die together.

When thou for sin rebukest man,
Forthwith he waxeth woe and wan:
Bitterness fills our bowels; all our hearts
     Pine, and decay,
     And drop away,
And carry with them the other parts.

But thou wilt sin and grief destroy;
That so the broken bones may joy,
And tune together in a well-set song,
     Full of his praises,
     Who dead men raises.
Fractures well cured make us more strong.

GH

AFFLICTION

Kill me not every day,
Thou Lord of life; since thy one death for me
Is more than all my deaths can be,
Though I in broken pay[4]
Die over each hour of Methusalem's stay.

If all men's tears were let
Into one common sewer, sea, and brine;
What were they all, compared to thine?
Wherein if they were set,
They would discolour thy most bloody sweat.

Thou art my grief alone,
Thou Lord conceal it not: and as thou art
All my delight, so all my smart:
Thy cross took up in one,
By way of imprest, all my future moan.

GH

CHAPELS OF EASE IN SLEEPLESSNESS

O eternal and most gracious God, who art able to make, and dost make the sick bed of thy servants, chapels of ease to them; and the dreams of thy servants, prayers and meditations upon thee: let not this continual watchfulness of mine, this inability to sleep, which thou hast laid upon me, be any disquiet, or discomfort to me, but rather an argument, that thou wouldst not have me sleep in thy presence.

What it may indicate or signify, concerning the state of my body, let them consider to whom that consideration belongs; do thou, who only art the Physician of my soul, tell her, that thou wilt afford her such defensives as that she shall wake ever towards thee, and yet ever sleep in thee; and that through all this sickness, thou wilt either preserve mine understanding from all decay and distractions, which these watchings might occasion, or that thou wilt reckon and account with me from before those violences, and not call any piece of my sickness, a sin.

JD

AFFLICTION

Broken in pieces all asunder,
  Lord, hunt me not,
  A thing forgot,
Once a poor creature, now a wonder,
  A wonder tortured in the space
  Betwixt this world and that of grace.

My thoughts are all a case of knives,
  Wounding my heart
  With scattered smart,
As watering pots give flowers their lives.
  Nothing their fury can control,
  While they do wound and prick my soul.

All my attendants are at strife,
  Quitting their place
  Unto my face:
Nothing performs the task of life:
  The elements are let loose to fight,
  And while I live, try out their right.

Oh help, my God! let not their plot
  Kill them and me,
  And also thee,
Who art my life: dissolve the knot,
  As the sun scatters by his light
  All the rebellions of the night.

Then shall those powers, which work for grief,
    Enter thy pay,
    And day by day
Labour for thy praise, and my relief;
    With care and courage building me,
    Till I reach heaven, and much more, thee.

GH

TRUE REPENTANCE

O eternal and most gracious God, the God of security, and the enemy of security too, who wouldst have us always sure of thy love, and yet wouldst have us always doing something for it: let me always so apprehend thee, as present with me, and yet to follow after thee, as though I had not apprehended thee . . .

Thou pardonest no sin so, as that that sinner can sin no more; thou makest no man so acceptable, as that thou makest him impeccable. Though therefore it were a diminution of the largeness, and derogatorily to the fullness of thy mercy, to look back upon those sins which in a true repentance I have buried in the wounds of thy Son, with a jealous or suspicious eye, as though they were now my sins, when I had so transferred them upon thy Son; as though they could now be raised to life again, to condemn me to death, when they are dead in him, who is the fountain of life; yet were it an irregular anticipation, and an insolent presumption, to think that thy present mercy extended to all my future sins, or that there were no embers, no coals of future sins left in me.

Temper therefore thy mercy so to my soul, O my God, that I may neither decline to any faintness of spirit, in suspecting thy mercy now to be less hearty, less sincere, than it used to be to those who are perfectly reconciled to thee; nor presume so of it, as either to think this present mercy an antidote against all poisons, and so expose my self to temptations upon confidence that this thy mercy shall preserve me, or that when I do cast my self into new sins, I may have new mercy at any time, because thou didst so easily afford me this.

JD

CONFESSION

Oh what a cunning guest
Is this same grief! Within my heart I made
    Closets; and in them many a chest;
    And like a master in my trade,
In those chests, boxes; in each box, a till:
Yet grief knows all, and enters when he will.

No screw, no piercer can
Into a piece of timber work and wind,
    As God's afflictions into man,
    When he a torture hath designed.
They are too subtle for the subtlest hearts;
And fall, like rheums,[5] upon the tenderest
  parts.

We are the earth; and they,
Like moles within us, heave, and cast about:
    And till they foot and clutch their prey,
    They never cool, much less give out.
No smith can make such locks but they have
  keys:
Closets are halls to them; and hearts, highways.

Only an open breast
Doth shut them out, so that they cannot enter;
    Or, if they enter, cannot rest,
    But quickly seek some new adventure.
Smooth open hearts no fastening have; but
  fiction
Doth give a hold and handle to affliction.

Wherefore my faults and sins,
Lord, I acknowledge; take thy plagues away:
For since confession pardon wins,
I challenge here the brightest day.
The clearest diamond: let them do their best,
They shall be thick and cloudy to my breast.

GH

COMPLAINING

Do not beguile my heart,
    Because thou art
My power and wisdom. Put me not to shame,
    Because I am
Thy clay that weeps, thy dust that calls.

    Thou art the Lord of glory:
      The deed and story
Are both thy due: but I a silly fly,
      That live or die
According as the weather falls.

    Art thou all justice, Lord?
      Shows not thy word
More attributes? Am I all throat or eye,
      To weep or cry?
Have I no parts but those of grief?

    Let not thy wrathful power
      Afflict my hour,
My inch of life: or let thy gracious power
      Contract my hour,
That I may climb and find relief.

GH

PERSEVERANCE

My God, the poor expressions of my love
Which warm these lines, and serve them up to
   thee
Are so, as for the present, I did move
  Or rather as thou movedst me.

But what shall issue, whether these my words
Shall help another, but my judgement be;
As a burst fowling-piece doth save the birds
  But kill the man, is sealed with thee.

For who can tell, though thou hast died to win
And wed my soul in glorious paradise;
Whether my many crimes and use of sin
  May yet forbid the banns[6] and bliss.

Only my soul hangs on thy promises
With face and hands clinging unto thy breast,
Clinging and crying, crying without cease
  Thou art my rock, thou art my rest.

                           GH

WILT THOU FORGIVE?

Wilt thou forgive that sin where I begun,
  Which was my sin, though it were done
    before?
Wilt thou forgive that sin, through which I run,
  And do run still: though still I do deplore?
    When thou hast done, thou hast not done,
      For I have more.

Wilt thou forgive that sin by which I have won
  Others to sin? and, made my sin their door?
Wilt thou forgive that sin which I did shun
  A year, or two: but wallowed in, a score?
    When thou hast done, thou hast not done,
      For I have more.

I have a sin of fear, that when I have spun
  My last thread, I shall perish on the shore;
But swear by thy self, that at my death thy Son
  Shall shine as he shines now, and heretofore;
    And, having done that, thou hast done,
      I fear no more.

JD

Such a Life, as Killeth Death

JUSTICE

     I cannot skill of these thy ways.
Lord thou didst make me, yet thou woundest
  me;
Lord, thou dost wound me, yet thou dost
  relieve me:
Lord, thou relievest, yet I die by thee.
Lord, thou dost kill me, yet thou dost reprieve
  me.
     But when I mark my life and praise,
     Thy justice me most fitly pays:
For, I do praise thee, yet I praise thee not:
My prayers mean thee, yet my prayers stray:
I would do well, yet sin the hand hath got:
My soul doth love thee, yet it loves delay.
     I cannot skill of these my ways.

GH

DEATH BE NOT PROUD

Death, be not proud, though some have called
    thee
Mighty and dreadful, for thou art not so:
For those who thou think'st thou dost
    overthrow
Die not, poor death; nor yet canst thou kill me.
From rest and sleep, which but thy picture be,
Much pleasure, then from thee much more
    must flow;
And soonest our best men with thee do go –
Rest of their bones and souls' delivery!
Thou'rt slave to fate, chance, kings, and
    desperate men,
And dost with poison, war, and sickness dwell;
And poppy or charms can make us sleep as
    well
And better than thy stroke. Why swell'st thou
    then?
One short sleep past, we wake eternally,
And death shall be no more: Death, thou shalt
    die!

JD

CAST DOWN

O most gracious God, who dost pursue and perfect thine own purposes, and dost not only remember me by the first accesses of this sickness, that I must die, but inform me by this further proceeding therein, that I may die now; by what steps and degrees soever it shall please thee to go, in the dissolution of this body, hasten O Lord that pace, and multiply O my God those degrees, in the exaltation of my Soul toward thee now, and to thee then.

My taste is not gone away, but gone up to sit at David's table, to taste, and see, that the Lord is good. My stomach is not gone, but gone up, so far upwards toward the Supper of the Lamb, with thy saints in heaven, as to the Table, to the communion of thy saints here in earth. My knees are weak, but weak therefore that I should easily fall to, and fix my self long upon my devotions to thee.

A sound heart is the life of the flesh; and a heart visited by thee, and directed to thee, by that visitation is a sound heart. There is no soundness in my flesh, because of thine anger; interpret thine own work, and call this sickness correction and not anger, and there is soundness in my flesh. There is no rest in my bones, because of my sin; transfer my sins, with which thou art so displeased, upon him with whom thou art so well pleased, Christ Jesus, and there will be rest in my bones.

And, O my God, who made thy self a light in a bush, in the midst of these brambles and thorns of a sharp sickness, appear unto me so, that I may see thee, and know thee to be my God, applying thy self to me even in these sharp and thorny passages.

Do this, O Lord, for his sake, who was not the less the King of Heaven, for thy suffering him to be crowned with thorns, in this world.

JD

40

PRAYER

Give my captive soul, or take
  My body also thither.
Another lift like this will make
  Them both to be together.

Before that sin turned flesh to stone,
  And all our lump to leaven;
A fervent sigh might well have blown
  Our innocent earth to heaven.

For sure when Adam did not know
  To sin, or sin to smother;
He might to heaven from Paradise go,
  As from one room to another.

Thou hast restored us to this ease
  By this thy heavenly blood;
Which I can go to, when I please,
  And leave the earth to their food.

GH

INTO THY HANDS

O eternal and most gracious God, who hast been pleased to speak to us, not only in the voice of Nature, who speaks in our hearts, and of thy word, which speaks to our ears, but in the speech of speechless Creatures, in Balaam's Ass, in the speech of unbelieving men, in the confession of Pilate, in the speech of the Devil himself, in the recognition and attestation of thy Son, I humbly accept thy voice, in the sound of this sad and funereal bell.

And first, I bless thy glorious name, that in this sound and voice, I can hear thy instructions, in another man's to consider mine own condition; and to know, that this bell which tolls for another, before it come to ring out, may take in me too. As death is the wages of sin, it is due to me; As death is the end of sickness, it belongs to me; And though so disobedient a servant as I, may be afraid to die, yet to so merciful a Master as thou, I cannot be afraid to come;

And therefore, into thy hands, O my God, I commend my spirit; A surrender, which I know thou wilt accept, whether I live or die; for thy servant David made it, when he put himself into thy protection for his life; and thy blessed Son made it, when he delivered up his soul at his death; declare thou thy will upon me, O Lord, for life or death, in thy time; receive my surrender of my self now, Into thy hands, O Lord I commend my spirit.

JD

AFFLICTION

My heart did heave, and there came forth, *O
    God!*
By that I knew that thou wast in the grief,
To guide and govern it to my relief,
    Making a sceptre of the rod:
        Hadst thou not had thy part,
Sure the unruly sigh had broke my heart.

But since thy breath gave me both life and
    shape,
Thou knowest my tallies; and when there's
    assigned
So much breath to a sigh, what's then behind?
    Or if some years with it escape,
        The sigh then only is
A gale to bring me sooner to my bliss.

Thy life on earth was grief, and thou art still
Constant unto it, making it to be
A point of honour, now to grieve in me,
    And in thy members suffer ill.
        They who lament one cross,
Thou dying daily, praise thee to thy loss.

GH

HYMN TO GOD MY GOD
IN MY SICKNESS

Since I am coming to that holy room,
   Where, with thy choir of saints for evermore,
I shall be made thy music; as I come
   I tune the instrument here at the door,
   And what I must do then, think here before.

Whilst my physicians by their love are grown
   Cosmographers, and I their map, who lie
Flat on this bed, that by them may be shown
   That this is my south-west discovery
   Per fretum febris, by these straits to die,

I joy, that in these straits, I see my west;
   For, though their currents yield return to none,
What shall my west hurt me? As west and east
   In all flat maps (and I am one) are one,
   So death doth touch the resurrection . . .

We think that Paradise and Calvary,
   Christ's Cross, and Adam's tree, stood in one
      place;
Look Lord, and find both Adams met in me;
   As the first Adam's sweat surrounds my face,
   May the last Adam's blood my soul embrace.

So, in his purple wrapped receive me Lord,
   By these his thorns give me his other crown;
And as to others' souls I preached thy word,
   Be this my text, my sermon to mine own,
   Therefore that he may raise the Lord throws
      down.

JD

44

A FUNERAL PRAYER

In the presence of God, we lay him down;
  In the power of God he shall rise;
  In the person of Christ, he is risen already.

And so into the same hands that have received his soul, we commend his body; beseeching his blessed Spirit, that as our charity enclines us to hope confidently of his good estate, our faith may assure us of the same happiness, in our own behalf;

And that for all our sakes, but especially for his own glory, he will be pleased to hasten the consummation of all, in that kingdom which that Son of God hath purchased for us, with the inestimable price of his incorruptible blood. Amen.

JD

LOVE

Thou art too hard for me in Love:
There is no dealing with thee in that art:
    That is thy masterpiece I see
    When I contrive and plot to prove
Something that may be conquest on my part,
    Thou still, O Lord, outstrippest me.

    Sometimes, when as I wash, I say,
And shrewdly, as I think, Lord, wash my soul
More spotted than my flesh can be.
    But then there comes into my way
Thy ancient baptism, which when I was foul
    And knew it not, yet cleansèd me.

I took a time when thou didst sleep
Great waves of trouble combating my breast:
    I thought it brave to praise thee then,
    Yet then I found, that thou didst creep
Into my heart with joy, giving more rest
    Than flesh did lend thee back again.

Let me but once the conquest have
Upon the matter 'twill thy conquest prove;
    If thou subdue mortality,
    Thou dost no more, than doth the grave:
Whereas, if I o'ercome thee and thy Love
    Hell, Death and Devil come short of me.

GH

SON OF GOD, HEAR US

Son of God hear us, and since thou
By taking our blood, owest it us again,
   Gain to thyself, or us allow;
And let not both us and thy self be slain;
   O Lamb of God, which took'st our sin
   Which could not stick to thee,
O let it not return to us again,
But patient and Physician being free,
As sin is nothing, let it no where be.

JD

SUPPLICATION AND PRESERVATION

Come, my Light, my Feast, my Strength:
Such a Light, as shows a feast:
Such a Feast, as mends at length:
Such a Strength, as makes his guest.

Such a Light, as Shows a Feast

MY DAILY BREAD

O eternal, and most gracious God, who gavest to thy servants in the wilderness, thy manna, bread so conditioned, qualified so, as that, to every man, manna tasted like that, which that man liked best . . . Thou wouldst have thy corrections taste of humiliation, but thou wouldst have them taste of consolation, too; taste of danger, but taste of assurance too.

As therefore thou hast imprinted in all thine elements, of which our bodies consist, two manifest qualities, so that, as thy fire dries, so it heats too; and as thy water moistens, so it cools too, so, O Lord, in these corrections, which are the elements of our regeneration, by which our souls are made thine, imprint thy two qualities, those two operations, that as they scourge us, they may scourge us into the way to thee: that when they have showed us, that we are nothing in our selves, they may also show us, that thou art all things unto us . . .

Let me think no degree of this thy correction casual, or without signification; but yet when I have read it in that language, as it is a correction, let me translate it into another, and read it as a mercy; and which of these is the original, and which is the translation, whether thy mercy, or thy correction, were thy primary, and original intention in this sickness, I cannot conclude, though death conclude me; for as it must necessarily appear to be a correction, so I can have no greater argument of thy mercy, than to die in thee, and by that death, to be united to him, who died for me.

JD

A PRAYER AFTER A SERMON

Blessed be God! and the Father of all mercy! who continueth to pour his benefits upon us. Thou hast elected us, thou hast called us, thou hast justified us, sanctified, and glorified us; Thou wast born for us, and thou livedst and diedst for us: Thou hast given us the blessings of this life, and of a better. Oh Lord! thy blessings hang in clusters, they come trooping upon us! they break forth like mighty waters on every side.

And now, Lord, thou hast fed us with the bread of life: so man did eat Angel's food: Oh Lord, bless it: Oh Lord, make it health and strength unto us; still striving and prospering so long within us, until our obedience reach the measure of thy love, who hast done for us as much as may be.

Grant this, dear Father, for thy Son's sake, our only Saviour: To whom with thee, and the Holy Ghost, three Persons, but one most glorious, incomprehensible God, be ascribed all Honour, and Glory, and Praise, ever. Amen.

GH

RESURRECTION

Moist with one drop of thy blood, my dry soul
Shall (though she now be in extreme degree
Too stony hard, and yet too fleshly), be
Freed by that drop, from being starved, hard,
     or foul,
And life, by this death abled, shall control
Death, whom thy death slew; nor shall to me
Fear of first or last death, bring misery,
If in thy little book my name thou enrol,
Flesh in that long sleep is not putrefied,
But made that there, of which, and for which
     'twas;
Nor can by other means be glorified.
May then sin's sleep, and death's soon from me
     pass,
That waked from both, I again risen may
Salute the last, and everlasting day.

JD

PRAYER

Of what an easy quick access,
My blessed Lord, art thou! how suddenly
    May our requests thine ear invade!
To show that state dislikes not easiness,
If I but lift mine eyes, my suit is made:
Thou canst no more not hear, than thou canst
    die.

Of what supreme almighty power
Is thy great arm which spans the east and west,
    And tacks the centre to the sphere!
By it do all things live their measured hour:
We cannot ask the thing, which is not there,
Blaming the shallowness of our request.

Of what immeasurable love
Art thou possessed, who, when thou couldst
    not die,
    Were fain to take our flesh and curse,
And for our sakes in person sin reprove,
That by destroying that which tied thy purse,
Thou might make sure for liberality!

Since then these three wait on thy throne,
Ease, *Power*, and *Love*; I value prayer so,
    That were I to leave all but one,
Wealth, fame, endowments, virtues, all should
    go;
I and dear prayer would together dwell,
And quickly gain, for each inch lost, an ell.[7]

GH

SACRAMENT

O eternal and most gracious God, who hast made little things to signify great, and conveyed the infinite merits of thy Son in the water of baptism, and in the bread and wine of thy other sacrament unto us: receive the sacrifice of my humble thanks, that thou hast not only afforded me the ability to rise out of this bed of weariness, but hast also made this bodily rising, by thy grace, an earnest of a second resurrection from sin, and of a third, to everlasting glory . . .

Thy good purposes upon me, I know, have their determination and perfection in thy holy will upon me; there thy grace is, and there I am altogether; but manifest them so unto me that I may not only have that comfort of knowing thee to be infinitely good, but that also of finding thee to be every day better and better to me . . .

Therefore I beg of thee my daily bread; and as thou gavest me the bread of sorrow for many days, and since the bread of hope for some, and this day the bread of possessing, in rising by that strength, which thou the God of all strength, hast infused into me, so, O Lord, continue to me the bread of life: the spiritual bread of life, in a faithful assurance in thee; the sacramental bread of life, in a worthy receiving of thee; and the more real bread of life, in an everlasting union to thee . . .

As my bodily strength is subject to every puff of wind, so is my spiritual strength to every blast of vanity. Keep me therefore still, O my gracious God, in such a proportion of both strengths, as I may still have something to thank thee for, which I have received, and still something to pray for, and ask at thy hand.

JD

THE ELIXIR

Teach me, my God and King,
In all things thee to see,
And what I do in anything,
To do it as for thee:

Not rudely, as a beast,
To run into an action;
But still to make thee prepossessed,
And give it its perfection.

A man that looks on glass,
On it may stay his eye;
Or if he pleaseth, through it pass,
And then the heav'n espy.

All may of thee partake:
Nothing can be so mean,
Which with this tincture (for thy sake)
Will not grow bright and clean.

A servant with this clause
Makes drudgery divine:
Who sweeps a room, as for thy laws,
Makes that and the action fine.

This is the famous stone
That turneth all to gold:
For that which God doth touch and own
Cannot for less be told.

GH

RENUNCIATION

We renounce, O Lord, all our confidence in this world; for this world passes away, and the lusts thereof. We renounce all our confidence in our own merits for we have done nothing in respect of that which we might have done; neither could we ever have done any such thing, but that still we must have remained unprofitable servants to thee. We renounce all confidence, even in our own confessions, and accusations of our self; for our sins are above number, if we would reckon them; above weight and measure, if we would weigh and measure them; and past finding out, if we would seek them in those dark corners in which we have multiplied them against thee. Yea, we renounce all confidence even in our repentances; for we have found by many lamentable experiences, that we never perform our promises to thee, never perfect our purposes in our selves, but relapse again and again into those sins which again and again we have repented.

We have no confidence in this world, but in him who hath taken possession of the next world for us, by sitting down at thy right hand. We have no confidence in our merits, but in him whose merits thou hast been pleased to accept for us, and to apply to us. We have no confidence in our own confessions and repentances, but in that blessed Spirit, who is the author of them, and loves to perfect his own works and build upon his own foundations.

Accept them therefore, O Lord, for their sakes

whose they are; our poor endeavours, for thy Son's
sake, in whom only our prayers are acceptable to
thee; and for thy Spirit's sake which is now in us,
and must be so whensoever we do pray acceptably
to thee; accept thou our humble prayers.

JD

Such a Feast, as Mends at Length

RECREATE ME

Father of Heaven, and him, by whom
It, and us for it, and all else, for us
   Thou madest, and govern'st ever, come
And recreate me, now grown ruinous:
      My heart is by dejection, clay,
       And by self-murder, red.
From this red earth, O Father, purge away
All vicious tinctures, that new fashionèd
I may rise up from death, before I'm dead.

                    JD

TRINITY SUNDAY

Lord, who hast formed me out of mud,
    And hast redeemed me through thy blood,
    And sanctified me to do good;

Purge all my sins done heretofore:
    For I confess my heavy score,
    And I will strive to sin no more.

Enright my heart, mouth, hands in me,
    With faith, with hope, with charity;
    That I may run, rise, rest with thee.

GH

MANY MANSIONS

O eternal, and most gracious God, who in thy upper house, the Heavens, though there be many mansions, yet art alike and equally in every mansion; but here in thy lower house, though thou fills all, yet art otherwise in some rooms thereof, than in others, otherwise in thy Church, than in my chamber, and otherwise in thy sacraments, than in my prayers; so though thou be always present, and always working in every room of this thy house, my body, yet I humbly beseech thee to manifest always a more effectual presence in my heart, than in the other Offices.

When thy blessed Son cried out to thee, My God, my God, why hast thou forsaken me, thou didst reach out thy hand to him; but not to deliver his sad soul, but to receive his holy soul; neither did he longer desire to hold it of thee, but to recommend it to thee.

I see thine hand upon me now, O Lord, and I ask not why it comes, what it intends; but a silent, and absolute obedience to thy will, even before I know it, is my cordial. Preserve that to me, O my God, and that will preserve me to thee; that when thou hast catechized me with affliction here, I may take a greater degree, and serve thee in a higher place, in thy kingdom of joy and glory. Amen.

JD

IN THY PASSION

O Son of God, who seeing two things,
Sin, and death crept in, which were never
    made,
  By bearing one, triedst with what stings
The other could thine heritage invade;
    O be thou nailed unto my heart,
      And crucified again,
Part not from it, though it from thee would
    part,
But let it be, by applying so thy pain,
Drowned in thy blood, and in thy passion slain.

JD

SHALL THY WORK DECAY?

Thou hast made me, and shall thy work decay?
Repair me now, for now mine end does haste,
I run to death, and death meets me as fast,
And all my pleasures are like yesterday;
I dare not move my dim eyes any way,
Despair behind, and death before does cast
Such terror, and my feeble flesh does waste
By sin in it, which it towards hell does weigh;
Only thou art above, and when towards thee
By thy leave I can look, I rise again;
But our old subtle foe so tempteth me,
That not one hour my self I can sustain;
Thy Grace may wing me to prevent his art,
And thou like Adamant[8] draw mine iron heart.

JD

THE SPIRITUAL PHYSICIAN

O most mighty, and most merciful God, who art so the God of health and strength as that without thee, all health is but the fuel, and all strength, but the bellows of sin; behold me under the vehemence of two diseases, and under the necessity of two physicians, authorized by thee, the bodily and the spiritual physician. I come to both, as to thine ordinance, and bless and glorify thy name, that in both cases, thou hast afforded help to man by the ministry of man . . .

Keep me back, O Lord, from them who misprofess arts of healing the soul, or of the body, by means not imprinted by thee in the Church for the soul, or not in nature for the body. There is no spiritual health to be had by superstition, nor bodily by witchcraft; thou Lord, and only thou art Lord of both. Thou in thy self art Lord of both, and thou in thy Son art the Physician, the applier of both. With his stripes we are healed, says the prophet. Before he was scourged, we were healed with his stripes; how much more shall I be healed now, when that which he hath already suffered actually, is actually and effectually applied to me?

Thou didst promise to heal the earth; but it is when the inhabitants of the earth pray that thou wouldst heal it. Thou didst promise to heal their waters; but their miry places, and standing waters, thou sayest there, thou wilt not heal: my returning to any sin, if I should return to the ability of sinning over all my sins again, thou wouldst not pardon. Heal this earth, O my God, by repentant tears, and heal these waters, these tears from all bitterness, from all diffidence, from all dejection, by establishing my irremovable assurance in thee.

Thy Son went about healing all manner of sicknesses, and will this universal Physician pass by this hospital, and not visit me? not heal me? not heal me wholly? If this day must remove me, till days shall be no more, seal to me, my spiritual health in affording me the seals of thy Church, and for my temporal health, prosper thine ordinance in their hands who shall assist in this sickness, in that manner, and in that measure as may most glorify thee, and most edify those who observe the issues of thy servants, to their own spiritual benefit.

JD

TEMPLE

    O Holy Ghost, whose temple I
Am, but of mud walls, and condensèd dust,
    And being sacrilegiously
Half wasted with youth's fires, of pride and
      lust,
        Must with new storms be weatherbeat;
        Double in my heart thy flame,
Which let devout sad tears intend; and let
(Though this glass lantern, flesh, do suffer
      maim)
Fire, Sacrifice, Priest, Altar be the same.

JD

NATURE

Full of rebellion, I would die,
Or fight, or travel, or deny
That thou hast ought to do with me.
            Oh tame my heart;
         It is thy highest art
To captivate strongholds to thee.

If thou shalt let this venom lurk,
And in suggestions fume and work,
My soul will turn to bubbles straight,
            And thence by kind
         Vanish into a wind,
Making thy workmanship deceit.

Oh smooth my rugged heart, and there
Engrave thy reverend law and fear;
Or make a new one, since the old
            Is sapless grown,
         And a much fitter stone
To hide my dust, than thee to hold.

GH

HOLY BAPTISM

Since, Lord, to thee
A narrow way and little gate
Is all the passage, on my infancy
Thou didst lay hold, and antedate
My faith in me.

Oh let me still
Write thee great God, and me a child:
Let me be soft and supple to thy will,
Small to myself, to others mild,
Behither ill.

Although by stealth
My flesh get on; yet let her sister
My soul bid nothing, but preserve her wealth:
The growth of flesh is but a blister;
Childhood is health.

GH

THE WINDOWS

Lord, how can man preach thy eternal word?
      He is a brittle crazy glass:
Yet in thy temple thou dost him afford
      This glorious and transcendent place,
      To be a window, through thy grace.

But when thou dost anneal in glass⁹ thy story,
      Making thy life to shine within
The holy Preacher's; then the light and glory
      More rev'rend grows, and more doth
        win:
      Which else shows wat'rish, bleak, and
        thin.

Doctrine and life, colours and light, in one
      When they combine and mingle, bring
A strong regard and awe: but speech alone
      Doth vanish like a flaring thing.
      And in the ear, not conscience ring.

GH

THY MERCY

O eternal, and most gracious God, who as thou givest all for nothing, if we consider any precedent merit in us, so givest nothing for nothing: if we consider the acknowledgement and thankfulness, which thou lookest for after, accept my humble thanks, both for thy mercy, and for this particular mercy, that in thy judgement I can discern thy mercy, and find comfort in thy corrections.

What a wretched, and disconsolate hermitage is that house, which is not visited by thee; and what a waif and stray is that man, that hath not thy marks upon him. These heats, O Lord, which thou hast brought upon this body, are but thy chafing of the wax, that thou might seal me to thee. These spots are but the letters, in which thou hast written thine own name, and conveyed thy self to me; whether for a present possession, by taking me now, or for a future reversion, by glorifying thy self in my stay here, I limit not, I condition not, I choose not, I wish not, no more than the house, or land that passes by any civil conveyance. Only be thou ever present to me, O my God, and this bed-chamber and thy bed-chamber shall be all one room, and the closing of these bodily eyes here, and the opening of the eyes of my soul, there, all one act.

JD

NEWNESS OF LIFE

O most Merciful Father, for thy most innocent Son's sake: and since he hath spread his arms upon the cross, to receive the whole world, O Lord, shut out none of us (who are now fallen before the throne of thy majesty and thy mercy) from the benefit of his merits; but with as many of us as begin their conversion and newness of life this minute, this minute, O God, begin thou thy account with them, and put all that is past out of thy remembrance. Accept our humble thanks for all thy mercies; and, continue and enlarge them upon the whole church.

JD

Such a Strength, as Makes his Guest

FROM A PRAYER BEFORE A SERMON

Blessed be the God of heaven and earth! who only doth wond'rous things. Awake therefore, my lute, and my viol! Awake all my powers to glorify thee! We praise thee! We bless thee! We magnify thee forever! And now, Oh Lord! in the power of thy victories, and in the ways of thy ordinances, and in the truth of thy love, lo, we stand here, beseeching thee to bless thy word, wherever spoken this day throughout the universal Church. Oh, make it a word of power and peace, to convert those who are not yet thine, and to confirm those that are. Particularly, bless it in this thy own kingdom, which thou hast made a land of light, a storehouse of thy treasures and mercies: oh, let not our foolish and unworthy hearts rob us of the continuance of this thy sweet love: but pardon our sins, and perfect what thou hast begun. Ride on, Lord, because of the word of truth, and meekness, and righteousness; and thy right hand shall teach thee terrible things.

Especially, bless this portion here assembled together, with thy unworthy servant speaking unto them: Lord Jesu! teach thou me, that I may teach them: sanctify, and enable all my powers; that in their full strength they may deliver thy message reverently, readily, faithfully, and fruitfully. Oh, make thy word a swift word, passing from the ear to the heart, from the heart to the life and conversation: that as the rain returns not empty, so neither may thy word, but accomplish that for which it is given. Oh Lord, hear! Oh Lord, forgive! Oh Lord, hearken! and do so for thy blessed Son's sake, in whose sweet and pleasing words, we say, *Our Father* . . .

GH

THE PASSION

Since blood is fittest, Lord, to write
Thy sorrows in, and bloody fight;
My heart hath store, write there, where in
One box doth lie both ink and sin:

That when sin spies so many foes,
Thy whips, thy nails, thy sounds, thy woes,
All come to lodge there, sin may say,
No room for me, and fly away.

Sin being gone, oh fill the place,
And keep possession with thy grace;
Lest sin take courage and return,
And all the writings blot or burn.

GH

THIS MINUTE

O eternal and most gracious God, I come to thy majesty with two prayers, two supplications.

I have meditated upon the jealousy which thou hast of thine own honour; and considered, that nothing can come nearer a violating of that honour, than to sue out thy pardon, and receive the seals of reconciliation to thee, and then return to that sin, for which I needed, and had thy pardon before. I know that this comes near to a making thy holy ordinances, thy word, thy sacraments, thy seals, thy grace, instruments of my spiritual fornications. Since therefore thy correction hath brought me to such a participation of thy self, to such an entire possession of thee, as that I durst deliver my self over to thee this minute: preserve me, O my God, from all relapses into those sins, which have induced thy former judgements upon me.

But because, by too lamentable experience, I know how slippery my customs of sin have made my ways of sin, I presume to add this petition too: that if my infirmity overtake me, thou forsake me not. Say to my soul, My son, thou hast sinned, do so no more; but say also, that though I do, thy spirit of remorse and compunction shall never depart from me.

Thy holy apostle, Saint Paul, was shipwrecked thrice and yet still saved. Though the rocks, and the sands, the heights, and the shallows, the prosperity, and the adversity of this world do diversely threaten me, though mine own leaks endanger me, yet, O God, let me never make shipwreck of faith

and a good conscience; and then thy long-lived, thy
everlasting mercy, will visit me, though that which
I most earnestly pray against should fall upon me, a
relapse into those sins which I have truly repented,
and thou hast fully pardoned.

JD

A SINNER IS MORE MUSIC

Hear us, O hear us Lord: to thee,
A sinner is more music, when he prays,
Than spheres, or Angels' praises be,
In Panegyric Alleluias;
Hear us, for till thou hear us, Lord
We know not what to say;
Thine ear to' our sighs, tears, thoughts give
voice and word.
O Thou who Satan heard'st in Job's sick day
Hear thyself now, for thou in us dost pray.

JD

SUBMISSION

But that thou are my wisdom, Lord,
    And both mine eyes are thine,
My mind would be extremely stirred
    For missing my design.

Were it not better to bestow
    Some place and power on me?
Then should thy praises with me grow,
    And share in my degree.

But when I thus dispute and grieve,
    I do resume my sight,
And pilfering what I once did give,
    Dispossess thee of thy right.

How know I, if thou shouldst me raise,
    That I should then raise thee?
Perhaps great places and thy praise
    Do not so well agree.

Wherefore unto my gift I stand;
    I will no more advise:
Only do thou lend me a hand,
    Since thou hast both mine eyes.

GH

DESIRE

O Eternal God, as thou didst admit thy faithful servant Abraham to make the granting of one petition an encouragement and rise to another, and gave him leave to gather upon thee from fifty to ten;[10] so I beseech thee, that since by thy grace I have thus long meditated upon thee and spoken of thee, I may now speak to thee. As thou hast enlightened and enlarged me to contemplate thy greatness, so, O God, descend thou and stoop down to see my infirmities and the Egypt in which I live; and (if thy good pleasure be such) hasten mine exodus and deliverance, for I desire to be dissolved, and be with thee.

JD

FEAR OF FEAR

O most mighty God and merciful God, the God of all true sorrow, and true joy too, of all fear, and of all hope too; as thou hast given me a repentance not to be repented of, so give me, O Lord, a fear, of which I may not be afraid. Give me tender, and supple, and conformable affections, that as I joy with them that joy, and mourn with them that mourn, so I may fear with them that fear.

And since thou has vouchsafed to discover to me, in his fear whom thou hast admitted to be my assistance, in this sickness, that there is danger therein, let me not, O Lord, go about to overcome the sense of that fear, so far, as to permit the fitting, and preparing of my self, for the worst that may be feared, the passage out of this life.

Many of thy blessed martyrs, have passed out of this life, without any show of fear; But thy most blessed Son himself did not so. Thy martyrs were known to be but men, and therefore it pleased thee, to fill them with thy Spirit, and thy power, in that they did more than men. Thy Son was declared by thee, and by himself to be God; and it was requisite, that he should declare himself to be man also, in the weaknesses of man. Let me not therefore, O my God, be ashamed of these fears, but let me feel them to determine, where his fear did, in a present submitting of all to thy will.

JD

I RESIGN MYSELF TO THEE

As due by many titles I resign
My self to thee, O God, first I was made
By thee, and for thee, and when I was decayed
Thy blood bought that, the which before was
    thine;
I am thy son, made with thy self to shine,
Thy servant, whose pains thou hast still repaid,
Thy sheep, thine image, and, till I betrayed
My self, a temple of thy Spirit divine:
Why does the devil then usurp on me?
Why does he steal, nay ravish that's thy right?
Except thou rise and for thine own work fight,
Oh I shall soon despair, when I do see
That thou lovest mankind well, yet wilt not
    choose me,
And Satan hates me, yet is loth to lose me.

JD

A CHURCH DEDICATION ON ASCENSION DAY

O Eternal, and most gracious God, Father of our Lord Jesus Christ; and in him, of all those that are his: As thou didst make him so much ours, as that he became like us, in all things, sin only excepted; make us so much his, as that we may be like him, even without the exception of sin, that all our sins may be buried in his wounds, and drowned in his blood.

And as this day we celebrate his Ascension to thee, be pleased to accept our endeavour of conforming our selves to his pattern, in raising this place for our ascension to him. Lean upon these pinnacles, O Lord, as thou didst upon Jacob's ladder, and hearken after us. Be this thine ark, and let thy dove, thy blessed Spirit, come in and out, at these windows: and let a full pot of thy manna, a good measure of thy word, and an effectual preaching thereof, be evermore preserved, and evermore be distributed in this place. Let the leprosy of superstition never enter within these walls, nor the hand of sacrilege ever fall upon them. And in these walls, to them that love profit and gain, manifest thou thy self as a treasure, and fill them so; to them that love pleasure, manifest thy self as marrow and fatness, and fill them so; and to them that love preferment, manifest thy self as a Kingdom, and fill them so; that so thou mayest be all unto all. Give thy self wholly to us all, and make us all wholly thine.

JD

ADORATION AND THANKSGIVING

Come, my Joy, my Love, my Heart:
Such a Joy, as none can move:
Such a Love, as none can part:
Such a heart, as joys in love.

Such a Joy, as None can Move

ANTIPHON

Let all the world in every corner sing,
    My God and King.

The heavens are not too high,
His praise may thither fly:
The earth is not too low,
His praises there may grow.

Let all the world in every corner sing,
    My God and King.

The church with psalms must shout,
No door can keep them out.
But above all, the heart
Must bear the longest part.

Let all the world in every corner sing,
    My God and King.

GH

ENLARGE OUR DAYS

Enlarge our days, O Lord, to that blessed day, prepare us before that day, seal us to that day, ratify to us after that day, all the days of our life, an assurance in that Kingdom, which thy Son our Saviour hath purchased for us, with the inestimable price of his incorruptible blood. To which glorious Son of God, with Thee and the Holy Spirit, be all honour and glory, now and forever. Amen.

JD

MATINS

I cannot ope mine eyes,
But thou art ready there to catch
My morning-soul and sacrifice:
Then we must needs for that day make a
match.

My God, what is a heart?
Silver, or gold, or precious stone,
Or star, or rainbow, or a part
Of all these things, or all of them in one?

My God, what is a heart,
That thou shouldst it so eye, and woo,
Pouring upon it all thy art,
As if that thou hadst nothing else to do?

Indeed man's whole estate
Amounts (and richly) to serve thee:
He did not heaven and earth create,
Yet studies them, not him by whom they be.

Teach me thy love to know;
That this new light, which now I see,
May both the work and workman show:
Then by a sunbeam I will climb to thee.

GH

GRATEFULNESS

Thou that hast given so much to me,
Give one thing more, a grateful heart.
See how thy beggar works on thee
     By art.

He makes thy gifts occasion more,
And says, If he in this be crossed,
All thou hast given him heretofore
     Is lost.

But thou didst reckon, when at first
Thy word our hearts and hands did crave,
What it would come to at the worst
     To save.

Perpetual knockings at thy door,
Tears sullying thy transparent rooms,
Gift upon gift, much would have more,
     And comes.

This notwithstanding, thou wentst on,
And didst allow us all our noise:
Nay, thou hast made a sigh and groan
     Thy joys.

Not that thou hast not still above
Much better tunes, than groans can make;
But that these country airs thy love
     Did take.

Wherefore I cry, and cry again;
And in no quiet canst thou be,
Till I a thankful heart obtain
      Of thee:

Not thankful, when it pleases me;
As if thy blessings had spare days:
But such a heart, whose pulse may be
      Thy praise.

GH

FUNERAL BELLS

O eternal and most gracious God, who having consecrated our living bodies, to thine own Spirit, and made us temples of the Holy Ghost, dost also require a respect to be given to these temples, even when the priest is gone out of them, to these bodies, when the soul is departed from them; I bless, and glorify thy Name, that as thou takest care in our life, of every hair of our head, so dost thou also of every grain of ashes after our death.

Neither dost thou only do good to us all, in life and death, but also wouldst have us do good to one another, as in a holy life, so in those things which accompany our death. In that contemplation I make account that I heard this dead brother of ours, who is now carried out to his burial, to speak to me, and to preach my funeral sermon, in the voice of these bells. In him, O God, thou hast accomplished to me, even the request of Dives to Abraham; thou hast sent one from the dead to speak unto me. He speaks to me aloud from that steeple; he whispers to me at these curtains, and he speaks thy words: Blessed are the dead which die in the Lord, from henceforth.

Let this prayer therefore, O my God, be as my last gasp, my expiring, my dying in thee; That if this be the hour of my transmigration, I may die the death of a sinner, drowned in my sins, in the blood of thy Son; And if I live longer, yet I may now die the death of the righteous, die to sin; which death is a resurrection to a new life. Thou killest and thou givest life; which soever comes, it comes from thee; which way soever it comes, let me come to thee.

JD

SION

Lord, with what glory wast thou served of old,
When Solomon's temple stood and flourishèd!
  Where most things were of purest gold;
  The wood was all embellishèd
With flowers and carvings, mystical and rare:
All showed the builder's, craved the seer's care.

Yet all this glory, all this pomp and state
Did not affect thee much, was not thy aim;
  Something there was, that sowed debate:
  Wherefore thou quitt'st thy ancient claim:
And now thy Architecture meets with sin;
For all thy frame and fabric is within.

There thou art struggling with a peevish heart,
Which sometimes crosses thee, thou sometimes
    it:
  The fight is hard on either part.
  Great God doth fight, he doth submit.
All Solomon's sea of brass and world of stone
Is not so dear to thee as one good groan.

And truly brass and stones are heavy things,
Tombs for the dead, not temples fit for thee:
  But groans are quick, and full of wings,
  And all their motions upward be;
And ever as they mount, like larks they sing;
The note is sad, yet music for a King.

GH

PRAYER

Prayer the Church's banquet, angels' age,
   God's breath in man returning to his birth,
   The soul in paraphrase, heart in pilgrimage,
The Christian plummet sounding heaven and
    earth;
Engine against the Almighty, sinners' tower,
   Reversèd thunder, Christ-side-piercing spear,
   The six-days' world transposing[11] in an hour,
A kind of tune, which all things hear and fear;
Softness, and peace, and joy, and love, and
    bliss,
   Exalted manna, gladness of the best,
   Heaven in ordinary, man well dressed,
The milky way, the bird of paradise,
Church-bells beyond the stars heard, the soul's
    blood,
The land of spices; something understood.

GH

EASTER

Rise heart; thy Lord is risen. Sing his praise
               Without delays,
Who takes thee by the hand, that thou likewise
               With him mayest rise:
That, as his death consignèd thee to dust,
His life may make thee gold, and much more
   just.

Awake, my lute, and struggle for thy part
               With all thy art.
The cross taught all wood to resound his name,
               Who bore the same.
His stretchèd sinews taught all strings, what
   key
Is best to celebrate this most high day.

Consort both heart and lute, and twist a song
               Pleasant and long:
Or since all music is but three parts vied
               And multiplied,
Oh let thy blessed Spirit bear a part,
And make up our defects with his sweet art.

GH

A WREATH

A wreathèd garland of deservèd praise,
Of praise deservèd, unto thee I give,
I give to thee, who knowest all my ways,
My crooked winding ways, wherein I live,
Wherein I die, not live: for life is straight,
Straight as a line, and ever tends to thee,
To thee, who art more far above deceit,
Than deceit seems above simplicity.
Give me simplicity, that I may live,
So live and like, that I may know thy ways,
Know them and practise them: then shall I give
For this poor wreath, give thee a crown of
      praise.

GH

PRAISE

Lord, I will mean and speak thy praise,
    Thy praise alone.
My busy heart shall spin it all my days:
  And when it stops for want of store,
Then will I wring it with a sigh or groan,
    That thou mayst yet have more.

When thou does favour any action,
    It runs, it flies:
All things concur to give it a perfection.
  That which had but two legs before,
When thou does bless, hath twelve: one wheel
    doth rise
    To twenty then, or more.

But when thou does on business blow,
    It hangs, it clogs:
Not all the teams of Albion[12] in a row
  Can hale or draw it out of door.
Legs are but stumps, and Pharaoh's wheels but
    logs,
  And struggling hinders more.

Thousands of things do thee employ
    In ruling all
This spacious globe: angels must have their joy,
  Devils their rod, the sea his shore,
The winds their stint: and yet when I did call,
    Thou heardst my call, and more.

I have not lost one single tear:
      But when mine eyes
Did weep to heaven, they found a bottle there
  (As we have boxes for the poor)
Ready to take them in; yet of a size
      That would contain much more.

But after thou hadst slipped a drop
      From thy right eye,
(Which there did hang like streamers near the
     top
  Of some fair church, to show the sore
And bloody battle which thou once didst try)
      The glass was full and more.

Wherefore I sing. Yet since my heart,
      Though pressed, runs thin;
Oh that I might some other hearts convert,
  And so take up at use good store:
That to thy chest there might be coming in
      Both all my praise, and more!

GH

ASCENSION

Salute the last and everlasting day,
Joy at the uprising of this sun, and son,
Ye whose just tears, or tribulation
Have purely washed, or burnt your drossy clay;
Behold the highest, parting hence away,
Lightens the dark clouds, which he treads
    upon,
Nor doth he by ascending, show alone,
But first he, and he first enters the way.
O strong ram, which hast battered heaven for
    me,
Mild lamb, which with thy blood, hast marked
    the path;
Bright torch, which shin'st, that I the way may
    see,
Oh, with thine own blood quench thine own
    just wrath,
And if thy Holy Spirit, my Muse did raise,
Deign at my hands this crown of prayer and
    praise.

JD

Such a Love, as None can Part

A WEDDING PRAYER

Lighten our darkness, we beseech thee, O Lord, that in thy light we may see light: illustrate our understandings, kindle our affections, pour oil to our zeal, that we may come to the marriage of this Lamb, and that this Lamb may come quickly to this marriage: and in the mean time bless these thy servants, with making this secular marriage a type of the spiritual, and the spiritual an earnest of that eternal, which they and we by thy mercy shall have in that kingdom, which thy Son our Saviour hath purchased with the inestimable price of his incorruptible blood. To whom with Thee and the Holy Spirit be glory everlasting. Amen.

JD

CLASPING OF HANDS

Lord, thou art mine, and I am thine,
If mine I am: and thine much more,
Than I or ought, or can be mine.
Yet to be thine, doth me restore;
So that again I now am mine,
And with advantage mine the more,
Since this being mine, brings with it thine,
And thou with me dost thee restore.
    If I without thee would be mine,
     I neither should be mine nor thine.

Lord, I am thine, and thou art mine:
So mine thou art, that something more
I may presume thee mine, than thine.
For thou didst suffer to restore
Not thee, but me, and to be mine,
And with advantage mine the more,
Since thou in death was none of thine,
Yet then as mine didst me restore.
    Oh be mine still! still make me thine!
    Or rather make no Thine and Mine!

GH

THE TEMPER

How should I praise thee, Lord! how should
   my rhymes
      Gladly engrave thy love in steel,
      If what my soul doth feel sometimes,
         My soul might ever feel!

Although there were some forty heavens, or
   more,
      Sometimes I peer above them all;
      Sometimes I hardly reach a score,
         Sometimes to hell I fall.

Oh rack me not to such a vast extent;
      Those distances belong to thee:
      The world's too little for thy tent,
         A grave too big for me.

Wilt thou meet arms with man, that thou dost
   stretch
      A crumb of dust from heaven to hell?
      Will great God measure with a wretch?
         Shall he thy stature spell?

Oh let me, when thy roof my soul hath hid,
      Oh let me roost and nestle there:
      Then of a sinner thou art rid,
         And I of hope and fear.

Yet take thy way; for sure thy way is best:
      Stretch or contract me, thy poor debtor:
      This is but tuning of my breast,
         To make the music better.

Whether I fly with angels, fall with dust,
Thy hands made both, and I am there:
Thy power and love, my love and trust
Make one place everywhere.

GH

THE FOUNTAIN OF ALL LIGHT

O eternal and most gracious God, who though thou didst permit darkness to be before light in the creation, yet in the making of light, didst so multiply that light, as that it enlightened not the day only, but the night too: though thou hast suffered some dimness, some clouds of sadness and disconsolateness to shed themselves upon my soul, I humbly bless, and thankfully glorify thy holy name, that thou hast afforded me the light of thy Spirit, against which the prince of darkness cannot prevail, nor hinder his illumination of our darkest nights, of our saddest thoughts.

Even the visitation of thy most blessed Spirit upon the blessed Virgin, is called an overshadowing. There was the presence of the Holy Ghost, the fountain of all light, and yet an overshadowing; nay, except there were some light, there could be no shadow. Let thy merciful providence so govern all in this sickness, that I never fall into utter darkness, ignorance of thee, or inconsideration of my self; and let those shadows which do fall upon me, faintness of spirit, and condemnations of my self, be overcome by the power of thine irresistible light, the God of consolation; that when those shadows have done their office upon me, to let me see that of my self, I should fall into irrecoverable darkness, thy Spirit may do his office upon those shadows, and disperse them, and establish me in so bright a day here, as may be a critical day to me, a day wherein, and whereby I may give thy judgement upon my self, and that the words of thy Son, spoken to his apostles, may reflect upon me, Behold, I am with you always, even to the end of the world.

JD

THE 23rd PSALM

The God of love my shepherd is,
    And he that doth me feed:
While he is mine, and I am his,
    What can I want or need?

He leads me to the tender grass,
    Where I both feed and rest;
Then to the streams that gently pass:
    In both I have the best.

Or if I stray, he doth convert
    And bring my mind in frame:
And all this not for my desert,
    But for his holy name.

Yea, in death's shady black abode
    Well may I walk, not fear:
For thou art with me; and thy rod
    To guide, thy staff to bear.

Nay, thou dost make me sit and dine,
    Ev'n in my enemy's sight:
My head with oil, my cup with wine
    Runs over day and night.

Surely thy sweet and wondrous love
    Shall measure all my days;
And as it never shall remove,
    So neither shall thy praise.

GH

THE WAY OF THY GLORY

O eternal and most gracious God, who though thou didst pass over infinite millions of generations, before thou came to a creation of this world, yet when thou began, didst never intermit that work, but continued day to day, till thou hadst perfected all the work, and deposed it in the hands and rest of a Sabbath; though thou hast been pleased to glorify thy self in a long exercise of my patience, with an expectation of thy declaration of thy self in this my sickness, yet since thou hast now of thy goodness afforded that which affords us some hope, if that be still the way of thy glory, proceed in that way, and perfect that work, and establish me in a Sabbath, and rest in thee, by this thy seal of bodily restitution.

But, O Lord, I am not weary of thy pace, nor weary of mine own patience. I provoke thee not with a prayer, not with a wish, not with a hope, to more haste than consists with thy purpose; nor look that any other thing should have entered into thy purpose, but thy glory. To hear thy steps coming towards me, is the same comfort, as to see thy face present with me. Whether thou do the work of a thousand years in a day, or extend the work of a day to a thousand years, as long as thou workest, it is light, and comfort. Heaven it self is but an extension of the same joy; and an extension of this mercy, to proceed at thy leisure, in the way of restitution, is a manifestation of heaven to me here upon earth . . .

As therefore the morning dew, is a pawn of the evening fatness, so, O Lord, let this day's comfort be the earnest of tomorrow's, so far as may conform me entirely to thee, to what end, and by what way soever thy mercy hast appointed me.

JD

EVENSONG

The day is spent, and hath his will on me:
  I and the sun have run our races,
  I went the slower, yet more paces,
    For I decay, not he.

Lord, make my losses up, and set me free:
  That I, who cannot now by day
  Look on his daring brightness, may
    Shine then more bright than he.

If thou defer this light, then shadow me:
  Lest that the night, earth's gloomy shade
  Fouling her nest, my earth invade,
    As if shades knew not thee.

But thou art light and darkness both together:
  If that be dark we cannot see,
  The sun is darker than a tree,
    And thou more dark than either.

Yet thou art not so dark, since I know this,
  But that my darkness may touch thine,
  And hope, that may teach it to shine,
    Since light thy darkness is.

Oh let my soul, whose keys I must deliver
  Into the hands of senseless dreams
  Which know not thee, suck in thy beams
    And wake with thee forever.

GH

EASTER WINGS

Lord, who createdst man in wealth and store,
    Though foolishly he lost the same,
        Decaying more and more,
            Till he became
                Most poor:
                With thee
            Oh let me rise
        As larks, harmoniously,
    And sing this day thy victories:
Then shall the fall further the flight in me.

My tender age in sorrow did begin:
    And still with sicknesses and shame
        Thou didst so punish sin,
            That I became
                Most thin.
                With thee
            Let me combine
        And feel this day thy victory:
    For, if I imp[13] my wing on thine,
Affliction shall advance the flight in me.

GH

THE WORLD'S LAST NIGHT

What if this present were the world's last night?
Mark in my heart, O Soul, where thou dost
    dwell,
The picture of Christ crucified, and tell
Whether that countenance can thee affright,
Tears in his eyes quench the amazing light,
Blood fills his frowns, which from his pierc'd
    head fell.
And can that tongue adjudge thee unto hell,
Which pray'd forgiveness for his foes' fierce
    spite?
No, no; but as in my idolatry
I said to all my profane mistresses,
Beauty, of pity, foulness only is
A sign of rigour: so I say to thee,
To wicked spirits are horrid shapes assign'd,
This beauteous form assures a piteous mind.

JD

Such a Heart, as Joys in Love

LOVE

Immortal Heat, Oh let thy greater flame
  Attract the lesser to it: let those fires,
  Which shall consume the world, first make it
    tame;
And kindle in our hearts such true desires,
As may consume our lusts, and make thee way.
  Then shall our hearts pant after thee; then
    shall our brain
  All her invention on thine Altar lay,
And there in hymns send back thy fire again.
Our eyes shall see thee, which before saw dust;
  Dust blown by wit, till that they both were
    blind:
  Thou shalt recover all thy goods in kind,
Who were dispossessed by usurping lust:
All knees shall bow to thee, all wits shall rise,
And praise him who did make and mend our
    eyes.

GH

EASTER

I got me flowers to straw thy way;
I got me boughs off many a tree:
But thou wast up by break of day,
And brought'st thy sweets along with thee.

The Sun arising in the East,
Though he give light, and the East perfume;
If they should offer to contest
With thy arising, they presume.

Can there be any day but this,
Though many suns to shine endeavour?
We count three hundred, but we miss:
There is but one, and that one ever.

GH

EVENSONG

Blest be the God of love,
Who gave me eyes, and light, and power this
day,
Both to be busy, and to play.
But much more blest be God above,
Who gave me sight alone,
Which to himself he did deny:
For when he sees my ways, I die:
But I have got his son, and he hath none.

What have I brought thee home
For this thy love? have I discharged the debt,
Which this day's favour did beget?
I ran; but all I brought, was foam.
Thy diet, care, and cost
Do end in bubbles, balls of wind;
Of wind to thee whom I have crossed
But balls of wildfire to my troubled mind.

Yet still thou goest on,
And now with darkness closest weary eyes,
Saying to man, It doth suffice:
Henceforth repose; your work is done.
Thus in thy ebony box[14]
Thou dost enclose us, till the day
Put our amendment in our way,
And give new wheels to our disordered clocks.

I muse, which shows more love,
The day or night: that is the gale, this th'
  harbour;
That is the walk, and this the arbour;
Or that the garden, this the grove.
My God, thou art all love.
Not one poor minute scapes thy breast,
But brings a favour from above;
And in this love, more than in bed, I rest.

GH

I WOULD BUT BLESS THY NAME

Eternal God, (for whom who ever dare
Seek new expression, do the Circle square,
And thrust into strait corners of poor wit
Thee, who art cornerless and infinite)
I would but bless thy Name, not name thee
    now;
(And thy gifts are as infinite as thou:)
Fix we our praises therefore on this one,
That, as thy blessed Spirit fell upon
These Psalms' first Author in a cloven tongue;
(For 'twas a double power by which he sung
The highest matter in the noblest form;)
So thou hast cleft that spirit, to perform
That work again, and shed it, here, upon
Two, by their bloods, and by thy Spirit one;
A Brother and a Sister, made by thee
The Organ, where thou art the Harmony.

JD

116

A TRUE HYMN

My joy, my life, my crown!
My heart was meaning all the day,
Somewhat it fain would say:
And still it runneth, mutt'ring up and down
With only this, *My joy, my life, my crown.*

Yet slight not these few words:
If truly said, they may take part
Among the best in art.
The fineness which a hymn or psalm affords,
Is, when the soul unto the lines accords.

He who craves all the mind,
And all the soul, and strength, and time,
If the words only rhyme,
Justly complains, that somewhat is behind
To make his verse, or write a hymn in kind.

Whereas if th'heart be moved,
Although the verse be somewhat scant,
God doth supply the want.
As when th'heart says (sighing to be approved)
Oh, could I love! and stops: God writeth, *Loved.*

GH

117

CHRISTMAS

The shepherds sing; and shall I silent be?
     My God, no hymn for thee?
My soul's a shepherd too; a flock it feeds
     Of thoughts, and words, and deeds.
The pasture is thy word: the streams, thy grace
     Enriching all the place.
Shepherd and flock shall sing, and all my
  powers
     Out-sing the daylight hours.
Then we will chide the sun for letting night
     Take up his place and right:
We sing one common Lord; wherefore he
  should
     Himself the candle hold.
I will go searching, till I find a sun
     Shall stay, till we have done;
A willing shiner, that shall shine as gladly,
     As frost-nipped suns look sadly.
Then we will sing, and shine all our own day,
     And one another pay:
His beams shall cheer my breast, and both so
  twine,
Till ev'n his beams sing, and my music shine.

GH

PRAISE

King of Glory, King of Peace,
      I will love thee.
And that love may never cease,
      I will move thee.

Thou has granted my request,
      Thou hast heard me:
Thou didst note my working breast,
      Thou hast spared me.

Wherefore with my utmost art
      I will sing thee,
And the cream of all my heart
      I will bring thee.

Though my sins against me cried,
      Thou didst clear me;
And alone, when they replied,
      Thou didst hear me.

Seven whole days, not one in seven,
      I will praise thee.
In my heart, though not in heaven,
      I can raise thee.

Thou grewest soft and moist with tears,
      Thou relentedst:
And when Justice called for fears,
      Thou dissentedst.

Small it is, in this poor sort
  To enroll thee:
Even eternity is too short
  To extol thee.

GH

BATTER MY HEART

Batter my heart, three person'd God; for, you
As yet but knock, breathe, shine, and seek to
   mend;
That I may rise, and stand, o'erthrow me, and
   bend
Your force, to break, blow, burn and make me
   new.
I, like an usurped town, to another due,
Labour to admit you, but Oh, to no end,
Reason your viceroy in me, me should defend,
But is captiv'd, and proves weak or untrue,
Yet dearly I love you, and would be loved fain,
But am betrothed unto your enemy:
Divorce me, untie, or break that knot again,
Take me to you, imprison me, for I
Except you enthral me, never shall be free,
Nor ever chaste, except you ravish me.

JD

EPILOGUE

I may Come to him with
my Prayer

And so as your eyes that stay here, and mine that must be far off, for all that distance shall meet every morning, in looking upon that same sun, and meet every night, in looking upon the same moon; so our hearts may meet morning and evening in that God, which sees and hears everywhere; that you may come thither to him with your prayers, that I, (if I may be of use for his glory, and your edification in this place) may be restored to you again; and [that] I may come to him with my prayer that what Paul soever plant amongst you, or what Apollos soever water, God himself will give us the increase:[15] That if I never meet you again till we have all passed the gate of death, yet in the gates of heaven, I may meet you all, and there say to my Saviour and your Saviour, that which he said to his Father and our Father, Of those whom thou hast given me, have I not lost one.

JOHN DONNE
Peroration of a Sermon of Valediction, April 18, 1619

Notes

Compiler's note:

The prayers and poems of John Donne and George Herbert passed through many editions in which numerous changes in the language and text were introduced. For the selections used in this compilation, standard texts were used, although most archaic spellings and punctuation have been updated. Certain of the materials, such as the prayers from *Devotions upon Emergent Occasions*, were originally untitled. In these cases, titles have been supplied from the texts themselves for the purpose of uniformity in this collection.

[1]*to be presented*   Under canon law, those who disturbed the services of the Church were to have their names 'presented' to the archdeacon or bishop upon their visitation.

[2]*cockatrice*   In legend this is said to be a serpent-like creature hatched from a cock's egg whose mere look could kill.

[3]*the Sicilian hill*   Indicating the actively volcanic Mount Etna.

[4]*in broken pay*   That is to say, 'in instalments'.

[5]*rheums*   Watery matter secreted from the mucous glands, once thought to cause disease upon contact.

[6]*banns*   The banns of marriage.

[7]*an ell*   An archaic measure of length, amounting to almost 45 inches.

[8]*Adamant*   A lodestone or magnet.

[9]*anneal in glass*   The process in stained glass work

whereby the colours are fixed to the glass by heat following the application of paint.

[10]Genesis 18.

[11]*transposing*   transforming

[12]*Albion*   An ancient name for England.

[13]*imp my wing*   A device of falconry whereby feathers are grafted into a damaged wing to restore the powers of flight.

[14]*in thy ebony box*   Vile or toxic liquids were thought to lose their poisonous qualities if kept in a box made of ebony wood.

[15]1 Corinthians 3.6.